I ♥ TRUMP

ADULT COLORING BOOK

COLOR TEST PAGE

CPAC

DONALD
TRUMP
FRAGRANCE

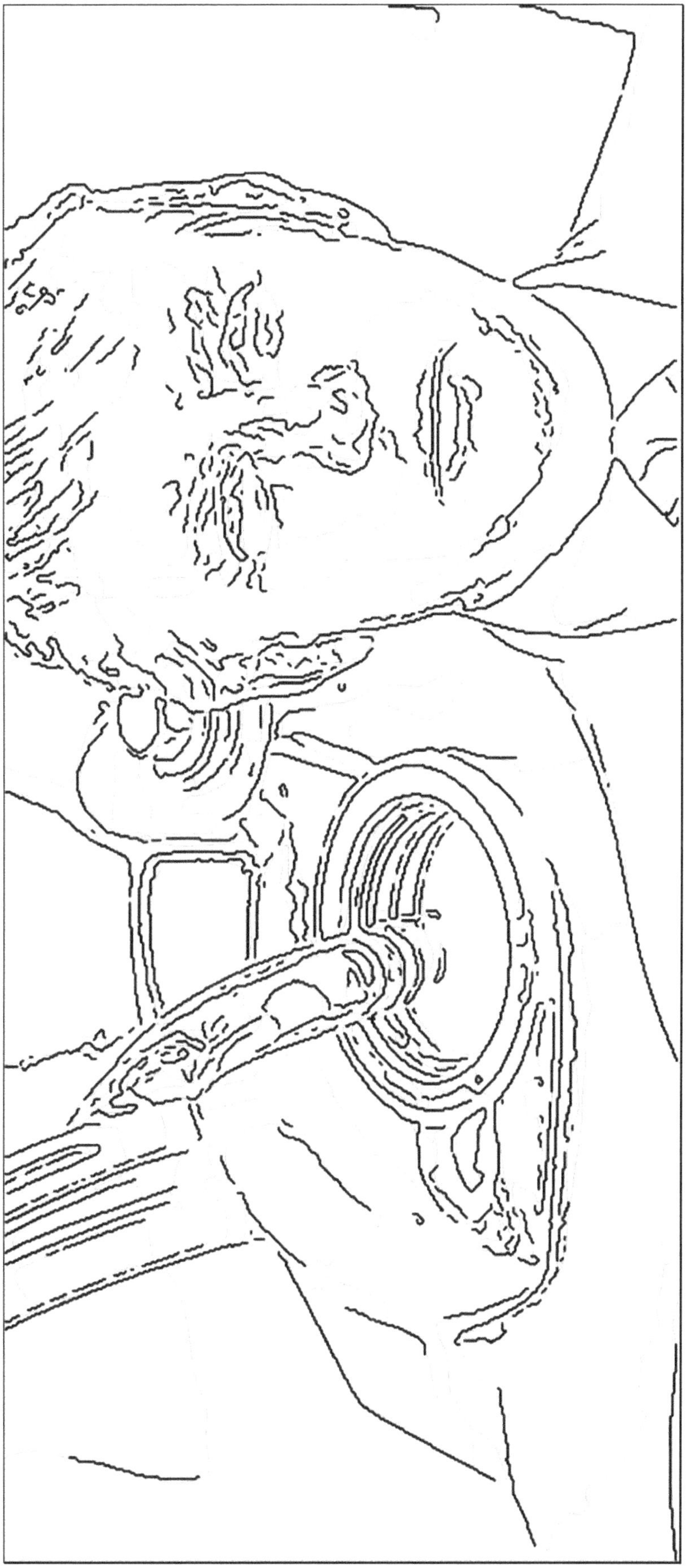

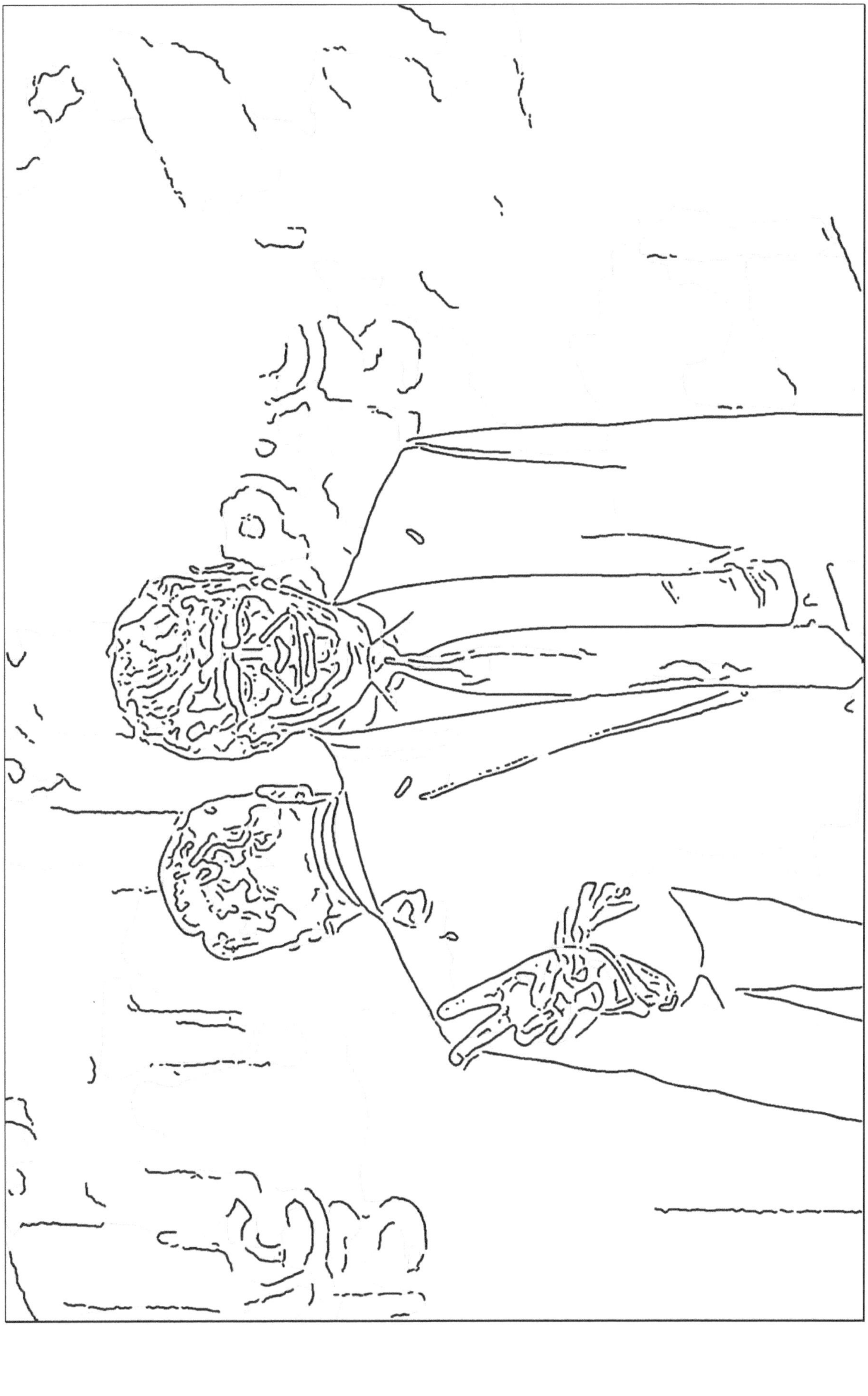

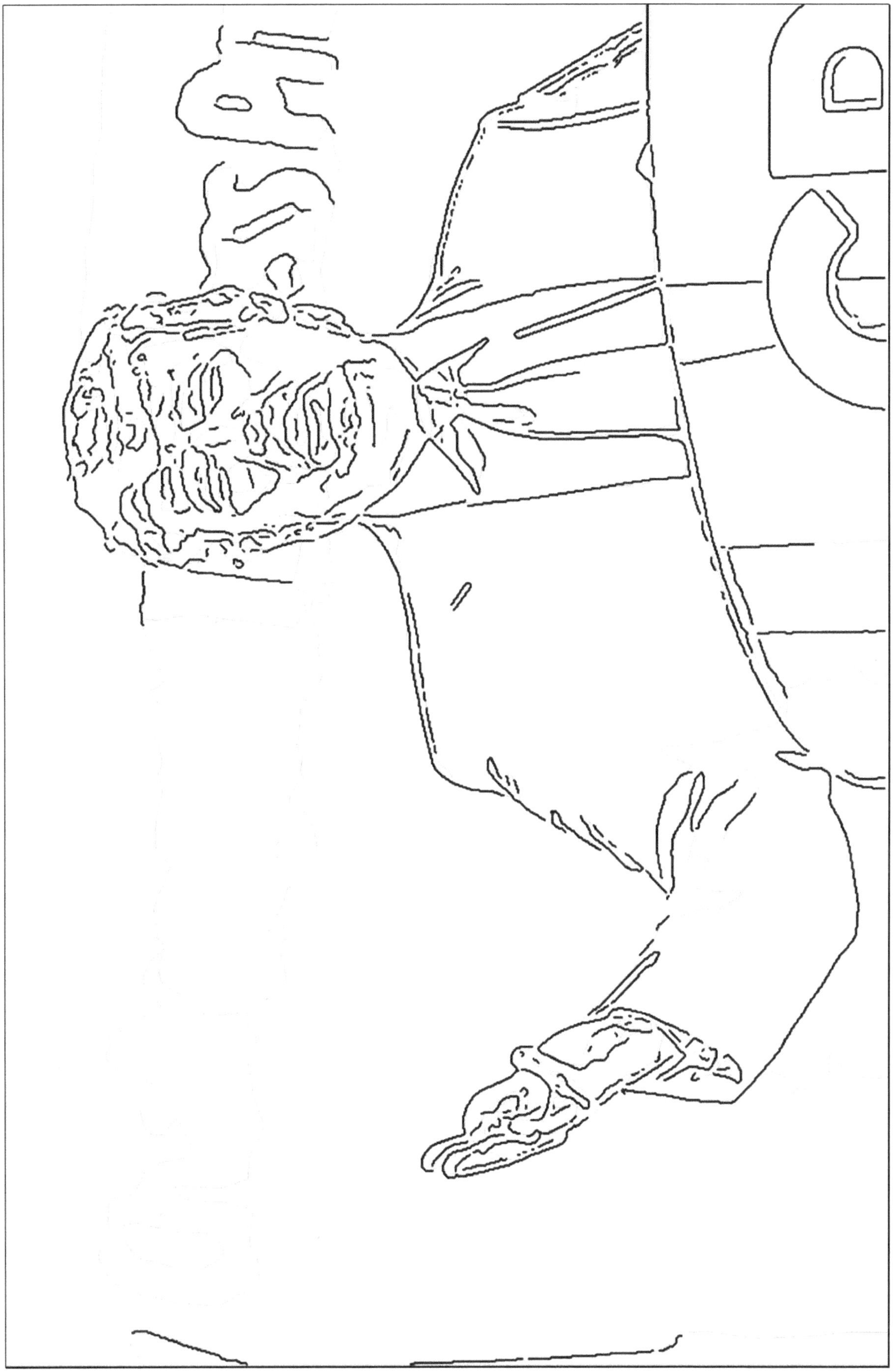

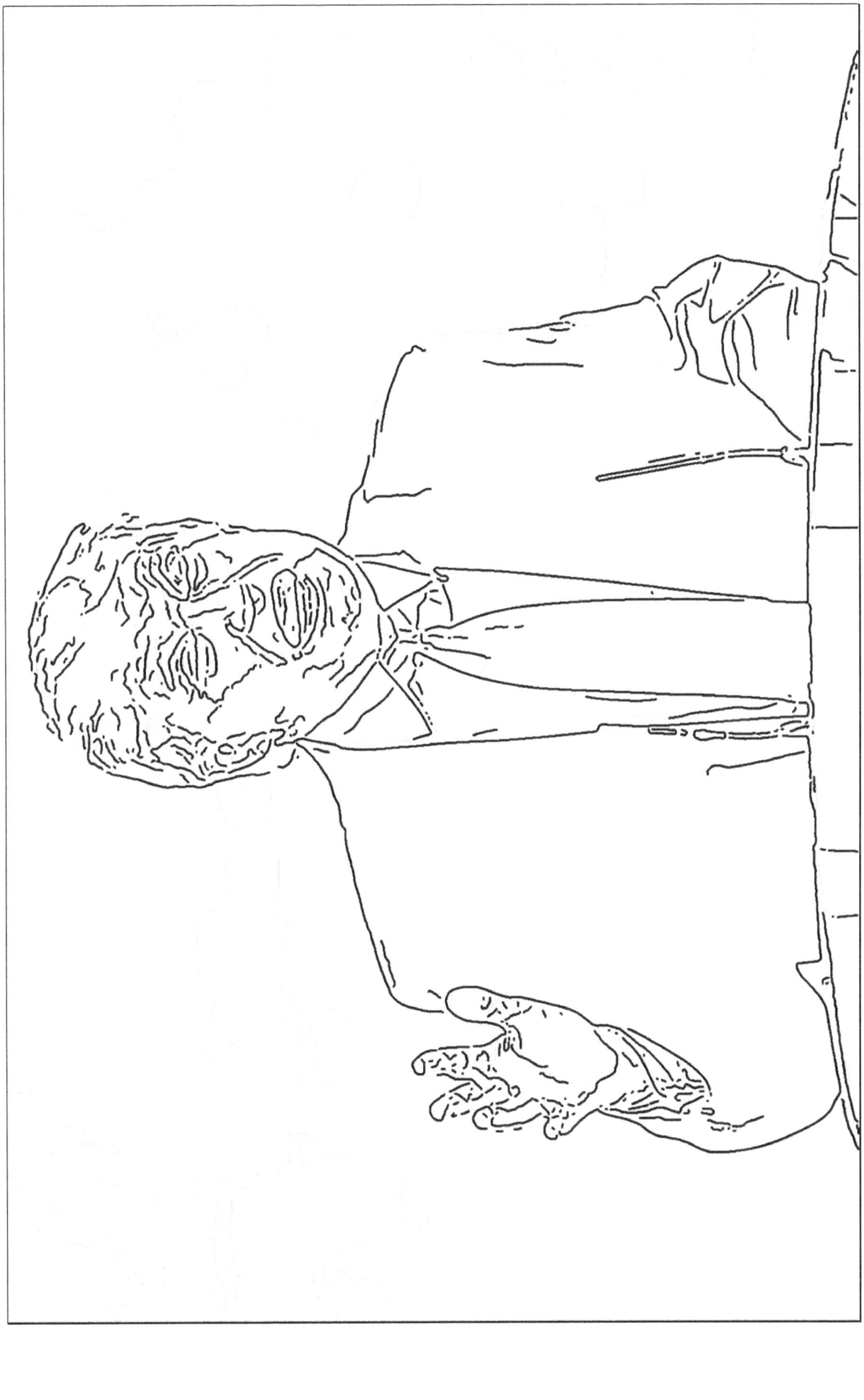

#FITN
REPUBLICAN LEADERSHIP SUMMIT

TRUMP
TRUMP

TRUMP

www.ingramcontent.com/pod-product-compliance
Lightning Source LLC
Chambersburg PA
CBHW081126280526
45787CB00007B/3001
* 9 7 8 1 5 3 5 0 0 0 4 4 4 *